A Wandering Walk Guide Book:

Pasadena, CA

Tom Alyea

NOTE:

The author has personally walked the route described in this book. Due to construction, street name changes, or any other factor it is possible that some of the directions may need to be revised as you take this self-guided tour and walk. A map has been included in this book to help you in the event the route has changed since the book was published.

CONTENTS

COLORADO STREET BRIDGE

TOURNAMENT OF ROSES PARADE IN PASADENA, CA

WALKING TOUR MAP

WALK DISTANCE: 8.0 MILES

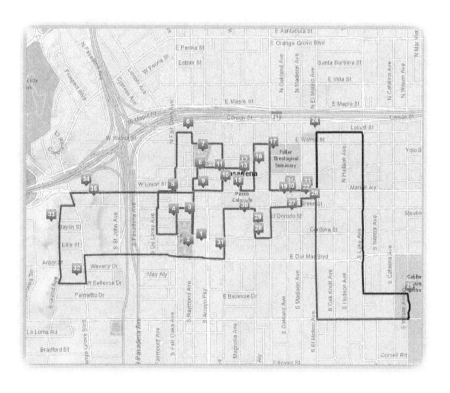

ROSE BOWL

> ➢ **Start your walking tour in front of the Del Mar Station in Pasadena, CA. This station is located at 230 S. Raymond St.**

Stop 1
Del Mar Station and Pasadena History
230 S. Raymond Avenue

Pasadena began as the San Gabriel Mission in 1771 when Spanish priests settled into the area after they were given a land grant by the Spanish government. In 1874, farmers from Indiana settled in the area and chose the name "Pasadena" which was a Native American word for "Crown of the Valley." The city is most famously known for its annual Tournament of Rose Parade that is held on New Year's Day. The parade has been held each year since 1890

The Pasadena Del Mar Station is part of the light-rail system in the Los Angeles Area. While most of what you see before you looks new, there are still remnants of the old Santa Fe Depot where the historic Super Chief trains used to stop on their way into Los Angeles and outbound towards Chicago. The original structure was designed in the old Southwestern style called Richardsonian Romanesque. Through a lot of effort, and the results of years of work, much of the station has been preserved or incorporated into the new structures you see around you.

> ➤ **Turn around and face Raymond Avenue for Stop 2.**

Stop 2
Pasadena Central Park
230 S. Raymond Avenue

This is one of the largest parks in Pasadena. It's a popular place for people to enjoy the year-round sun, play a little lawn bowling, and take the kids to enjoy the playground equipment.

> ➤ **Facing Central Park and Raymond Avenue, turn RIGHT for Stop 3.**

Stop 3
Hotel Green
99 S. Raymond Avenue

The Hotel Green is one of the oldest hotels in Pasadena. George Green started building the hotel in 1893 to serve the wealthy tourists coming to California. Most hotel guests arrived at the Santa Fe Railroad Depot, which was just down the street. In 1898, and again in 1903, Green expanded the hotel complex. The Hotel Green became the social and cultural center for Pasadena in the late 1800s. The historic Valley Hunt Club and the Tournament of Roses Association met inside the hotel for many years.

At one time there was a pedestrian bridge that crossed over Raymond Avenue. It was a popular viewing location for the Rose Parade which use to run along Raymond Avenue.

> ➢ **Continue on S. Raymond Avenue.**
> ➢ **LEFT on E. Green St.**
> ➢ **LEFT on S. Fair Oaks Avenue to Stop 4.**

Stop 4
Hotel Carver
107 S. Fair Oaks Avenue

This Victorian-era building has quite a history. It was built in the 1880s as a showroom for a stage coach company. When trains started coming to Pasadena, the building was transformed into a freight depot warehouse.

In the early 1900's, the building was converted into the Hotel Mikado, which was one of the first hotels to serve the Japanese-American community in the LA area. Then, in the 1940's, Percy Carter purchased the hotel. It became the first hotel owned by an African-American in Pasadena. While the Hotel Green across the street served white clientele, the Hotel Carver, which was named after scientist George Washington Carver, served the black community.

The Hotel Carver remained a hotel until the 1970s when it was once again converted, this time into artist studios.

> ➤ Continue on S. Fair Oaks Avenue.
> ➤ RIGHT on W. Valley St.
> ➤ RIGHT on S. de Lacey Avenue.
> ➤ RIGHT on W. Colorado Blvd. for Stop 5.

Stop 5
Tournament of Roses Parade
Colorado Boulevard

Imagine it's January 1 and there are over 700,000 people lining this street. That's what it's like each year on New Year's Day when the Tournament of Roses Parade heads down Colorado Boulevard. The first Parade was held in 1890 when members of the Pasadena Valley Hunt Club wanted to showcase the mild winters in California to their friends back in the East Coast. Although the floats weren't as elaborate back then, there were still carriages covered in flowers of all kinds. A few years later, marching bands and the first mechanical floats were added to the Parade. After about 5 years of managing the Parade, the Valley Hunt Club found it to be too much work, so the Pasadena Tournament of Roses Association was formed. Today, the Association's home is at the stately Wrigley Mansion, which you will see later on the tour.

Here are some interesting things to know about the Tournament of Roses Parade:

- All floats on the Parade must be completely covered in natural materials, such as flowers, seeds, bark, etc..
- The Valley Hunt Club still enters a flower-decorated carriage each year.
- It takes about a year to design and construct each float, although the natural materials aren't placed on the floats until a few days before the Parade.
- 24 different awards are given out each year with expert judges making the decision on who receives which award.
- Each year a Grand Marshal is selected to lead off the Parade. Some of the more notable Grand Marshal's include Pres. Dwight D. Eisenhower, Walt Disney, John Wayne, Bob Hope, and George Lucas.
- It takes over 65,000 hours of manpower each year for the volunteers to just keep things running smoothly for the Parade.
- The first Parade in 1890 had 2,000 people lining the Parade route. The highest number was over 1,000,000 people in 2004 and over 70 million watched the Parade live on TV.

> ➤ **Continue on W. Colorado Blvd.**
> ➤ **LEFT on Fair Oaks Avenue.**
> ➤ **RIGHT on Chestnut St. to Stop 6**

Stop 6
St. Andrew's Catholic Church
311 N. Raymond Avenue

St. Andrew's Church is the oldest Catholic parish in Pasadena and one of the oldest in the Los Angeles area. The parish was founded in 1886. The current church building you see before you was finished in 1927. Its Romanesque Revival campanile bell tower can be seen around the area for many miles away. The style of the church is modeled after the historic Basilica of St. Sabina in Rome, Italy.

Prior to building the church, the architect, Ross Montgomery, and the church's senior pastor, Monsigner John McCarthy traveled to Rome to study Byzantine architecture. After visiting St. Sabina, they knew this was the style of church they wanted built back in California.

Inside the church you will find beautiful murals painted by Italian painter, Carlo Wostry. He spent five years of his life working on the interior decorations of St. Andrew's.

> ➢ **Right on N. Raymond St.**
> ➢ **LEFT on Walnut St. to Stop 7.**

Stop 7
Levitt Pavilion for Performing Arts
87 N. Raymond Avenue

This historic bandshell was constructed in 1930. The outdoor performing arts venue brings together the community of Pasadena each year to listen to free summer concerts.

The Levitt Pavilion is located in Memorial Park. This Park was originally called Library Park because Pasadena's first library once stood near where the Pavilion now sits. That library was damaged in a 1933 earthquake and removed in 1954.

You can see local, emerging talent along with award-winning performers at the Levitt each year. The concerts are free, so you just need to bring a chair or blanket to enjoy the performances.

> ➤ **Continue on Walnut St.**
> ➤ **RIGHT on N. Marengo Avenue.**
> ➤ **RIGHT on Holly St. to Stop 8.**

Stop 8
Holly Street Livery Stable
110 E. Holly St.

In 1904, John Breiner built this stable for the horse and wagons he needed to deliver groceries throughout the Pasadena area. Breiner was the owner of the Pasadena City Market. The building has a unique trapezoid shape because it was situated right next to the railroad tracks on each side of the building. The railroad was critical for Breiner as it brought in many of the products he needed in his grocery business.

Once automobiles and trucks came along there wasn't a need for a stable. The building was converted into a number of different functions. It once housed stables for horses used in the Rose Parade as well as a construction site for floats.

> ➤ **Continue on Holly St.**
> ➤ **LEFT on N. Legge Alley.**
> ➤ **RIGHT on E. Union St.**
> ➤ **LEFT on N. Raymond Avenue**
> ➤ **LEFT on E. Colorado Blvd to stop 9.**

Stop 9
Chamber of Commerce Building
117 E. Colorado Blvd.

This building, which once housed the Pasadena Chamber of Commerce, was built in 1904.

You are now walking through what is called "Old Pasadena." This was the original commercial and shopping district for Pasadena. Many of the buildings in this area were constructed in the early 1900's.

Its hard to believe, but in the 1970's, this area was a run-down district with little more than empty shells for buildings and most of the people walking the streers were drug dealers or the homeless. In the 1980's and 1990's, redevelopment plans were created and this once prosperous area of Pasadena has returned back to its glory.

> ➤ **Continue on Colorado Blvd.**
> ➤ **LEFT on N. Marengo Avenue to Stop 10.**

Stop 10
MacArthur Building
24 N. Marengo Avenue

This historic building in downtown Pasadena was built in 1926. The Art-Deco inspired building continues as office spaces for various companies.

> ➢ **Continue on N. Marengo Avenue to Stop 11.**

Stop 11
First Baptist Church
75 N. Marengo Avenue

This ornate building is home to the First Baptist Church of Pasadena.

> ➢ **Continue on N. Marengo Avenue.**
> ➢ **RIGHT on N. Holly St to Stop 12.**

Stop 12
Pasadena City Hall
100 N. Garfield Avenue

You are looking at what may be one of the most beautiful city hall buildings in the entire US. The Pasadena City Hall was completed in 1927 at a cost of over $1.3 million to construct. The architectural style is a blending of the Mediterranean Revival Style and the Spanish Colonial Revival style. There are over 230 rooms inside this city government building.

Being so close to Hollywood, this building has been in a number of different films and television shows. It was portrayed as an embassy in the "Mission: Impossible" TV series and used as a villa in the 1940 film "The Great Dictator," by Charlie Chaplin. It's most recent portrayal can be seen outside the window of the main characters' apartment in the TV show "The Big Bang Theory."

No need to worry about earthquakes with this building. In 2004 the entire building was lifted off its foundation and earthquake stabilizers added to a new foundation.

> ➢ **RIGHT on N. Garfield Avenue and look for Stop 13.**

Stop 13
Robinson Memorial
100 N. Garfield Avenue

This memorial is a tribute to two of the most famous residents who once lived in Pasadena – Jackie and Mack Robinson.

Jackie Robinson was the first African-American to play in major league baseball. Fittingly, his bust faces towards the East where he played in Brooklyn, NY for the Dodgers.

Mack Robinson was a star athlete for the University of Oregon and went on to compete in the 1936 Olympics in Berlin, Germany. During those games he won a silver medal in the 200-meter sprint race – just behind Jesse Owens. Mack returned back to Pasadena in his later years and worked for the city of Pasadena. He lost his job with the city in retaliation for black people going to court to desegregate the swimming pools. That is why his bust faces City Hall as a reminder of his stance on civil rights.

> ➢ **Continue on N. Garfield to Stop 14.**

Stop 14
US Post Office
281 E. Colorado Avenue

This is one of the most ornate and beautiful US Post Office buildings in the entire LA area.

> ➤ **LEFT on E. Colorado Avenue.**
> ➤ **LEFT on N. Euclid Avenue to Stop 15.**

Stop 15
All Saint's Episcopal Church
132 N. Euclid Avenue

This English Gothic style church is home to the parish of All Saints Episcopal. This parish was founded in 1882 when eleven people met for the first time in the home of Mr. C.C. Brown. This is the third building for the congregation and it was completed in 1924.

The congregation of this church is one of the most liberal in the Southern California area. It has a history of social activism that dates back to the 1960's. When churches seemed to ignore the racial issues in the LA area, this church was one of the first to start speaking out about injustices African Americans were having within the city. It's rector at that time, John Burt, even joined Dr. Martin Luther King, Jr. to speak in LA in 1964. In the 1970's, the congregation was anti-Vietnam War, in the 80's the church created the first AIDS Center in the city, and in the 90's the first same-sex union blessing was given inside this church.

> ➢ **Continue on N. Euclid Ave.**
> ➢ **RIGHT on Walnut St.**
> ➢ **RIGHT on N. Los Robles Avenue to Stop 16.**

Stop 16
First Congregational Church
464 E. Walnut St.

The congregation of the First Congregational Church of Pasadena (also known as the Church of Christ), first began holding services in 1885. This church building is the third church in for the congregation and was completed in 1927. Today, the congregation has closed much of the building as it awaits new owners.

➢ **Continue on N. Los Robles to Stop 17.**

Stop 17
USC Pacific Asia Museum
46 N. Los Robles Avenue

This 1926 building was designed to replicate the style of a Chinese imperial palace, including having a central courtyard, decorative carvings, and a small pool with gardens.

The USC Pacific Asia Museum started as the Grace Nicholson Treasure House of Oriental Art in 1943. That was when Ms. Nicholson donated the building and many of the original art pieces she had collected. The museum became part of the University of Southern California in 2013.

Inside, you will find more than 15,000 rare and extremely beautiful art pieces from throughout Asia and the Pacific Islands.

> ➢ **Continue on N. Los Robles Ave.**
> ➢ **LEFT on E. Colorado Avenue to Stop 18.**

Stop 18
Route 66
E. Colorado Avenue

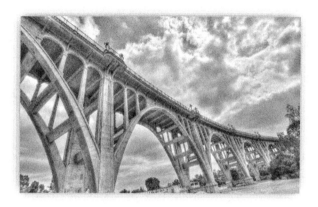

As you walk along Colorado Avenue you are also seeing a bit of a "blast from the past." This section of road through Pasadena is part of famous Route 66 that extends from Chicago, IL all the way to Santa Monica, CA.

One of the more famous features of Route 66 not too far from here is the beautifully designed, and very ornate, Colorado Street Bridge. With arches that soar 150' above the Arroyo Seco, it was the largest, and highest, concrete bridge for many years when it was first built in 1913.

> ➤ **Continue on E. Colorado Ave. to Stop 19.**

Stop 19
First United Methodist Church
500 E. Colorado Avenue

This beautiful church on Colorado Avenue was built in 1924. It is home to the congregation of First United Methodist Church. The church which was founded in the 1870's.

Inside the church you will find an original E.M. Skinner pipe organ and beautiful stained glass windows from Tiffany Studios.

> ➤ **Continue on E. Colorado Ave. to Stop 20.**

Stop 20
Singer Building
520 E. Colorado Avenue

During the 1920's, the Spanish Colonial Revival design style was all the rage in Southern California. This building, designed by architect Everett Babcock, is one of the few remaining buildings of this style remaining in Pasadena. This building was constructed as a showroom for the Singer Sewing Machine Company in 1926.

Some of the more prominent features of the Spanish Colonial style include the red tiled roof, stone friezes in a tiled pattern, and ornate piers with decorative moldings. All of these features are very noticeable on the outside of the Singer Building.

> ➤ **Continue on E. Colorado Ave. to Stop 21.**

Stop 21
Star-News Building
525 E. Colorado Avenue

This building once made radio history. Shortly after this Beaux Arts style building was constructed in 1925 for radio station KPSN, two large radio towers that once sat on top of this building broadcast the first Rose Parade in 1926.

This building was financed by the *Pasadena Star-News* newspaper. That paper began publishing back in 1883. The newspaper printing presses continued to run from this building until the late 1990's, when the Star-News moved to another location. The building was purchased by Glabman's Furniture and has since held a number of retail and office spaces.

➤ **Continue on E. Colorado Ave. to Stop 22.**

Stop 22
United Artist Theater
600 E. Colorado Avenue

This Art Deco style theater building was built in 1932. It once housed a single movie screen theater for United Artists. It remained a theater until the 1980's when the space was converted to retail shops.

This theater often acted as a test site for specialized sound and projection equipment that United Artists wanted to try out in its theaters across the U.S.

> ➤ **Continue on E. Colorado Ave. to Stop 23.**

Stop 23
First Trust Building
611 E. Colorado Avenue

The First Trust Building, also known as Lloyd's Bank, was constructed in 1927.

What is most notable about this building is that a professor from Caltech, R.R. Martel, designed an innovative earthquake-proof support system during a renovation of this building in the 2000's. His design used steel beams and girders, along with reinforcing concrete, to make the building safe in the event of an earthquake This was the first time those construction methods were used to keep a building safe in a major quake. This became an important advancement in securing building to prevent earthquake damage that is be used in renovations today.

> ➤ **Continue on E. Colorado Ave.**
> ➤ **LEFT on N. el Molino Ave to Stop 24.**

Stop 24
Theodore Parker Lukens House
266 N. el Molino Avenue

Theodore Lukens is best known as a charter member of the Sierra Club and was a good friend of John Muir. He played a significant role in the club's early activities in the LA area in the late 1800's. He also was a noted horticulturalist and major real estate investor in Pasadena. One of Luken's major environmental activities was his attempt to introduce reforestation efforts to California in the 1890's. Because of his efforts, a lake and a mountain are named for him.

This home was built in 1887 and is one of the oldest standing homes left in Pasadena. This Victorian-era home was built with elements of the Queen Anne style of architecture.

> ➤ **Continue on N. el Molino Avenue.**
> ➤ **RIGHT on Locust St.**
> ➤ **RIGHT on N. Lake Avenue.**
> ➤ **LEFT on San Pasqual St. to Stop 25.**

Stop 25
California Institute of Technology
1200 E. California Blvd.

You are about to begin walking through parts of the California Institute of Technology, most commonly known as Caltech. Caltech is ranked as one of the world's top-ten universities with a focus on the natural sciences and engineering. Caltech was founded as a vocational school in 1891 by Amos Throop. At last count, Caltech alumni counted for 73 Nobel Laureates.

Here are some interesting facts about Caltech:

- The mascot and team name for Caltech sports is the Beavers.
- Female undergraduates weren't allowed to attend courses until 1970.
- Most of the students are apolitical and weren't involved in any of the protests during the 60's and 70's. The only organized protest occurred in 1968 when it was

rumored that NBC was going to cancel the "Star Trek" TV series.

- Caltech is not a state institution. It is a private corporation.
- It's pretty tough to get into Caltech. You have to have some of the highest SAT and ACT test scores in the nation. Even then only about 6.5% of those who apply will be admitted. There are less than 1000 undergrad students and only about 1200 doing graduate level work.
- Pranks are part of the tradition with Caltech students. The most famous was when students covered parts of the famous Hollywood sign so it read "Caltech."
- Many notable scientists have graduated from Caltech. The most noted was Eugene Shoemaker who discovered the comet Shoemaker-Levy which crashed into the planet Jupiter. He is also the first person to be buried on the moon – his ashes were crashed landed there by a rocket.
- The honor code is so strong at Caltech that most exams are take-home where students can do their tests in a more comfortable environment.
- Another famous tradition is senior "Ditch Day." This is a day where seniors skip classes and leave behind elaborate traps and tasks that freshmen must undertake to get out of their dorm rooms. Some seniors spend months devising the best ways to lock students in their rooms.

Note: The campus is fun to explore and you're invited to walk around the buildings anytime you want. Just return back to this spot to continue on your Wandering Walk.

> ➤ **RIGHT on S. Wilson Avenue.**
> ➤ **RIGHT on E. California Blvd.**
> ➤ **RIGHT on S. El Molino Avenue to Stop 26.**

Stop 26
Pasadena Playhouse
39 S. El Molino Avenue

The Pasadena Playhouse had its first performance inside this historic Spanish Colonial Revival style building in 1925. The Playhouse had its beginning in the period know as the "Little Theatre Movement" that spread across cities and towns in the US in the early 1900's. This was a wave of regional style performances in smaller venues that allowed people who couldn't travel to Broadway in New York to see a play or musical.

For a period of time, the Pasadena Playhouse also operated a school of theatre arts that became an accredited college in 1937. This school lasted until the 1960's when more schools and universities opened up drama departments around the US. Actors, such as Raymond Burr, Gene Hackman, Charles Bronson, Dustin Hoffman, and Sally Struthers all learned their acting skills here. The Pasadena Playhouse also operated one of the first television stations in Southern California.

> ➢ **Continue on S. El Molino Ave.**
> ➢ **LEFT on Playhouse Alley.**
> ➢ **LEFT on S. Madison Ave.**
> ➢ **RIGHT on E. Green St. to Stop 27.**

Stop 27
First Church Christ, Scientist
550 E. Green St.

This church was built in 1909 and at the time of its completion it was the largest building in Pasadena. The building was specifically designed to be totally fireproof and the concrete dome on top of the building was one of the first in Pasadena.

> ➢ **LEFT on Los Robles Avenue.**
> ➢ **RIGHT on Cordova Street.**
> ➢ **RIGHT on S. Euclid Avenue for Stop 28.**

Stop 28
Masonic Temple
200 S. Euclid Avenue

This monumental Beaux-Arts style building was completed in 1927. In fact, it is the only example of the Beaux-Arts architecture style that exists in Pasadena today. The architect of the building was Cyril Bennett. Bennett designed many of the buildings you see in Pasadena, but this was one of his crowning achievements.

The first meeting of the Masons occurred in Pasadena in 1883. They would eventually form Pasadena Lodge No. 272.

The interior of the building is quite majestic and much of the building today is used as an event space. Inside you will find decorative marble and woodwork crafted in a fashion you can't find today.

> ➤ **Continue on S. Euclid Avenue to Stop 29.**

Stop 29
Miss Orton's Classical School for Girls
154 S. Euclid Avenue

Miss Orton's was the first non-religious private girls' school in Pasadena. Opening in 1890, it remained the best girls' school until 1913. Miss Orton's School was a pioneer of women's education in the city during that time. This was not just a fancy finishing school where young women learned to become good wives and mothers. It was an academically oriented school where young ladies actually had a chance at a real education that would allow them to further their education at colleges on the East Coast. The school eventually closed in 1930.

The first building constructed for educator Anna Orton, was a small, single classroom in 1892. A few years later a larger gymnasium was constructed along with a large Victorian Colonial Revival style dormitory. The dormitory is one of the last structures left of the former school.

> ➤ **Continue on S. Euclid Avenue.**
> ➤ **LEFT on E. Green St. to Stop 30.**

Stop 30
Pasadena Convention Center and Civic Auditorium
300 E. Green St.

The Pasadena Convention Center has had quite a bit of history inside its walls since it was first built in 1932. The site consists of three buildings: An Exhibition Building, a Conference Building, and a large 3,000 seat Civic Auditorium that hosts musicals, concerts, operas, and TV specials.

The building is best known as the site of the Emmy Awards from 1977-1997. It has also hosted such specials as "America's Got Talent," the "Miss Teen USA Pageant", and is home to the annual "People's Choice Awards."

In 1983, during the taping of "Motown 25: Yesterday, Today, Forever" special, Michael Jackson performed his hit song "Billie Jean." During his performance he introduced his signature dance move, the "Moonwalk" for the very first time.

> ➤ **Continue on E. Green St.**
> ➤ **LEFT on Marengo Avenue to Stop 31.**

Stop 31
Stoutenburgh House
255 S. Marengo Ave.

This beautiful Queen Anne home was built for John and Mary Stoutenburgh in 1893. It was one of the few remaining homes of this style left in the Pasadena area.

> ➤ **Continue on S. Marengo Avenue.**
> ➤ **RIGHT on E. Del Mar Blvd.**
> ➤ **LEFT on S. Orange Grove Blvd to Stop 32.**

Stop 32
Wrigley Mansion
391 S. Orange Grove Blvd.

In 1932, William Wrigley Jr, founder of Wrigley Gum Company, acquired this 16,000 square foot mansion in Pasadena. It was called his Winter "Cottage." This Spanish Colonial style home has 24 rooms and 12 bathrooms and was built in 1914. This was the smallest of Wrigley's homes. His other homes in Chicago, Philadelphia, and Catalina Island were all much larger.

Today, this mansion is known as "Tournament House," because the Pasadena Tournament of Roses Association has its corporate offices here. Mrs. Wrigley loved this home because she could watch the Rose Parade from her front lawn. When she died in 1958, she gave the home to the Roses Association with the explicit instructions that it was to be used as their offices.

You can tour the home and, along with viewing beautiful furnishings and seeing the gardens, you can see trophy's and other memorabilia from the Tournament of Roses Parades over the years.

> ➤ **Continue on S. Orange Grove Blvd.**
> ➤ **RIGHT on Lockehaven St.**
> ➤ **RIGHT on Grand Avenue to Stop 33.**

Stop 33
Richard H. Chambers Courthouse
125 S. Grand Avenue

This building has had quite a varied history since construction was completed in 1920. It began life as the Vista del Arroyo Hotel. During World War II, it was transformed into the McCornack General Hospital. Since then it has been used as a general-purpose federal government building and today houses the Richard H. Chambers US Court of Appeals.

The courthouse portion of the building is the largest of several buildings within the entire complex. It is designed in the Spanish Colonial Revival style with the tower, which was completed in 1930, being the centerpiece of the building. The dome of the tower is covered in multi-colored tiles and is quite beautiful for a government building.

> ➤ **Continue on S. Grand Avenue.**
> ➤ **RIGHT on Green St.**
> ➤ **LEFT on Orange Grove Blvd.**
> ➤ **RIGHT on W. Colorado Blvd to Stop 34.**

Stop 34
Norton Simon Museum of Art
411 W. Colorado Blvd.

The Norton Simon Museum, also known as the Pasadena Art Museum, began in 1953 with a collection of pieces donated by collector Galka Scheyer. The Pasadena Art Museum began collecting more pieces over the years and eventually opened a small museum close to the downtown area. In 1969, The Pasadena Art Museum built this modernistic style building. The distinctive exterior is covered in over 115,000 glazed tiles.

In the 1970's, the museum experienced some financial difficulties and billionaire industrialist Norton Simon donated his collection of art objects, and a considerable amount of money, to help keep the museum operational. Today, this highly acclaimed museum has over 11,000 permanent art objects.

> ➤ **Continue on W. Colorado Blvd to Stop 35.**

Stop 35
Elks Lodge No. 672
400 W. Colorado Blvd.

In 1911, the Elks fraternal organization built this lodge building for meetings and other events. It is still used regularly by the Elks.

> ➤ **Continue on W. Colorado Blvd to S. Raymond St.**
> ➤ **RIGHT on S. Raymond St. to end your walk in Pasadena.**

While in Pasadena, you can also visit these other great sites and attractions

The Gamble House
4 Westmoreland Pl, Pasadena, CA 91103

This historic landmark, which is owned and operated by the University of Southern California, is an excellent example of American Arts and Crafts style architecture. Tours are provided on a daily basis.

Eaton Canyon
1750 N Altadena Dr, Pasadena, CA 91107

A beautiful park right at the feet of the Sierra Madre, no entrance fee, good for level hiking and mountain hiking. The nature path instructs on plants and animals in the area. There are facilities for a cookout and shelters. Parking area closes at 5 pm, but you can stay in the park longer.

Jet Propulsion Laboratory
4800 Oak Grove Dr, Pasadena, CA 91109

To get a great understanding of how are space programs in the US operate, visiting the Jet Propulsion Laboratory is a must see. Be aware, you must register on-line and make a reservation way in advance, but it's well worth it. You can learn about the history of JPL, view the super clean assembly facilities and the mission control center for all un-manned (robotic) interplanetary flights (Houston Mission Control only handles space flights with humans aboard). Guests can only visit as part of a group guided tour. Very nice museum as well.

Rose Bowl Stadium
1001 Rose Bowl Dr, Pasadena, CA 91103

This famous stadium is the home of one of America's most popular annual college football games.

Kidspace Children's Museum
480 N Arroyo Blvd, Brookside Park, Pasadena, CA 91103

One of Southern California's most awesome family destinations, the Kidspace Children's Museum is located on over 3.5 acres and has more than 40 hands-on exhibits, as well as daily interactive activities and programs.

The Huntington Library, Art Collections and Botanical Gardens
1151 Oxford Rd, San Marino, CA 91108

This 207 acre complex houses a library, art collection and stunning gardens. The library and art gallery contain rare books and one of the most complete collections of 18th century art outside of London.

Notes

_____

_____

_____

_____

_____

_____

_____

_____

_____

_____

_____

_____

_____

Notes

_____

_____

_____

_____

_____

_____

_____

_____

_____

_____

_____

_____

_____

_____

_____

Notes

Notes

_____

_____

_____

_____

_____

_____

_____

_____

_____

_____

_____

_____

_____

_____

_____

_____